FRANCES AND THE HOUNDS OF DARKNESS

and

MOON MADNESS

two stories by
Joan Carlyon

CAMBRIDGE
UNIVERSITY PRESS

Published by the Press Syndicate of the University of Cambridge,
The Pitt Building, Trumpington Street, Cambridge CB2 1RP
40 West 20th Street, New York, NY 10011-4211, USA
10 Stamford Road, Oakleigh, Victoria 3166, Australia

First published 1992

Printed in Great Britain at the University Press, Cambridge

A catalogue record for this book is available from the British
Library

ISBN 0 521 43865 9

Illustrated by Lis Watkins

Prepared by *specialist publishing services* 090 857 307

Other titles available in the Moonstones series include:

The Downhill – Stephanie Baudet
The Farnbury Frogs – Kay McManus
Good Terms – Maggie Paun
Peter and the Pear Pond – Joan Carlyon
The Riddle of the Stone – Joan Carlyon
Secrets and Shadows – Joan Carlyon
The Wishing Seat – Anne de Menezes

JSS, 943.
£2.95.

Frances and the Hounds of Darkness

Chapter 1

Frances wriggled and stared at the ceiling. This was her first ever visit to her cousins' house and she wasn't liking it one bit. Until a month ago she had lived happily in Northern Ireland and now she had come to live in England – "across the water" as her grandmother referred to it.

Mum and Aunt Moira were talking, twenty to the dozen, about their families and there was plenty to hear and tell. They hadn't seen each other for a long time.

Frances had been lumbered with her cousin, Patrick. Aunt Moira had asked him to show Frances the family photograph album, which he'd done in about thirty seconds flat. Now he was amusing himself by carefully pulling the wings off a struggling fly which had landed on the table in front of him.

Patrick was casting sly glances at Frances, watching for her reactions. She was trying to ignore him but the angry buzzing inside her head was growing louder. In her imagination she conjured up a huge, hairy spider which hung, suspended from a fine thread above Patrick's head. The spider was so enormous that Frances half hoped that its thread would snap, causing it to fall and crush her cousin to a pulp. She decided that plan B was better – the one where the spider dismembers Patrick before eating him slowly.

"Isn't she sweet," crooned Aunt Moira, as if she'd noticed Frances for the first time. "Won't you look at that red hair, isn't it something?"

"Yeah, ginger string," muttered Patrick, flicking the remains of the fly at his cousin. "I'm off out, Mum. 'Bye Aunt Geraldine, see you."

"But, Patrick ..." Aunt Moira's voice trailed off as Patrick went out, slamming the door behind him.

"I'm sorry about Pat. He's been acting funny lately. He misses his dad.

"Now then, Frances," she continued. "I've made a fresh raspberry trifle for tea. I hope you'll like it."

Frances was staring at the ceiling but the spider had gone. She had trouble keeping her apparitions once her anger had disappeared. She often tried to hang on to her anger but had decided it's a bit like being happy – you either are or you aren't. It's not something you can fake.

"Frances, Auntie Moira is talking to you. You look as if you're expecting the roof to fall in," said Mum, impatiently.

Frances turned quickly and looked at her aunt, who was glancing anxiously at the ceiling and then back at her.

"Sorry, Aunt. What was it you said? I didn't quite catch it," said Frances meekly. Unlike Patrick and the fly, she thought, with disgust.

"Do you like raspberry trifle? It's tea-time. I cannot imagine why Patrick has gone off."

I wondered what the nasty smell was, thought Frances, wrinkling up her nose. She didn't like to suggest that Patrick had probably gone off to kill a cat or mug a mouse, so she smiled politely and answered, "Yes, thank you, Auntie Moira, I love raspberry trifle."

The table was set and tea was ready but Patrick had not returned.

"Frances, would you be a darling and pop upstairs and wake Joe?" asked Aunt Moira. "He's had a good nap and should be ready for his tea now. He's an angel child, that one. He and Patrick are like chalk and cheese."

Frances agreed. She had only been in the MacGuire household for two hours but already she had sorted out the sheep from the goats. Little Joe was a lamb but Patrick was one of those belligerent old billy goats that goes around head-butting everything.

She tiptoed upstairs and quietly opened the door of Joe's bedroom, hoping to wake him gently. But she needn't have worried. Joe was wide awake, playing and crooning to himself. He looked up at her and his eyes widened with pleasure. Scrambling to his feet he steadied himself against the bars of the cot and held up his arms to Frances.

"Hello, darling Joe," she crooned, "aren't you the lovely one. Come to cousin Frances and we'll go and have some tea."

Joe gurgled and laughed while Frances carefully carried him downstairs.

Mum offered to help, and she was given the job of changing Joe's nappy. Frances was very glad that she hadn't been roped in, but her relief turned to irritation when Aunt Moira asked her if she would pop into the garden to find Patrick.

"He's most likely down behind the shed," said Aunt Moira. "He spends hours hanging about down there. He misses his dad, you know."

Trying to show willing, Frances went out into the garden.

It isn't much of a garden, she thought, glancing around, although it's tidy enough.

The grass was neatly cut but, apart from a few straggling

raspberry bushes, nothing much was growing. She could see the shed at the bottom end of the garden, between a high fence and a big, old pear tree.

Before searching behind the shed, Frances stood near the house and looked around. What that tree needs is a tree house, she thought. It was the perfect place to hide, and from that height it would be just right for looking across to the woods which she had seen from the window in Joe's room.

A flurry of leaves, high in the tree, caught her attention as something small fell from the branches. Frances hurried to the end of the garden to see what it was. She was almost at the shed when she stopped dead. Patrick appeared from behind the shed. He was also searching for whatever had fallen out of the tree. Head down, Patrick didn't notice Frances run up. She was about to ask him what he was looking for, but stopped when she saw what he was carrying. It was a catapult.

Frances knew at once what was lying beneath the tree and her anger exploded inside her. The noise in her head was like the rush of mighty wings. Before she turned to run away Frances pictured a huge eagle, beak and talons at the ready, hovering above Patrick's head.

When Mum eventually found Frances she was furious with her.

"Where have you been?" said Mrs Riley in an angry whisper. "You knew that tea was ready ages ago. What are you doing in Joe's room? You were sent to find Patrick and he's been indoors for quarter of an hour now. We were beginning to worry that something nasty had happened."

Frances didn't say anything. Something nasty had happened but there was nothing anyone could do about it. She got up from behind Joe's cot where she'd been sitting and followed Mum downstairs. She wanted to go home.

Chapter 2

A month had passed since the visit to her cousins and Frances had almost forgotten the diabolical Patrick. She was settling in at her new school and had made friends with a girl called Kerry. They were in the same class and, as if to make life almost perfect, she and Kerry lived on the same housing estate.

Frances had another reason for feeling especially happy with her new life. She was the proud owner of a golden hamster, named Christabel. Frances had bought her with some birthday money. She had spent a long time choosing one of the soft balls of fur which were snuggled together in the pet shop cage.

The real surprise came a few days later. Christabel gave birth to six babies and Frances watched with amazement and delight as the mini-miracle took place before her eyes. Mum was a little alarmed. Christabel was very young and Mum was afraid she might eat her young. There was no need to worry. Christabel was all set to be a caring mother and so the next problem was how to accommodate so many hamsters.

"This could turn out to be a very complicated multiplication sum," said Mum, when she realised that all of the hamsters were going to survive. "I think you had better find homes for Christabel's babies, Frances, and quickly. Hamsters grow very fast and after four weeks they will be reproducing if you don't separate them."

Frances still felt like a new girl at school but she was gradually making friends with her classmates. One break-time, soon after the birth, she told Kerry that Mum wanted her to find homes for the young hamsters as soon as possible.

"I don't want to give Christabel's babies to just anybody. I want them to be properly cared for. They are kind of special," she added.

"Don't worry, Frances, I've just had an ace brain-wave!" said Kerry. "Why don't we print out some adoption papers and anyone who is interested will have to fill out the form and sign it to say that they promise, no – that they swear – to give proper love and care to their hamster?"

"That's brilliant, Kerry! And we could get them to prick their thumbs with a pin and put their thumb print in blood, to make it a sort of a solemn oath."

Frances grinned. "I'll ask Mum, tonight, if we can use her word processor. That will make it look really important and official," she said, very pleased with herself.

Mum helped the girls to type the document. She felt that it was a good idea to set out the *do's* and *don'ts* of keeping hamsters but she wasn't too keen on the thumb print. It all seemed a bit blood-thirsty. And, as she pointed out, it wasn't very hygienic. If the new owners all got infected thumbs they wouldn't be much good at handling their hamsters.

The girls carried out their plan and, in a very short time, five of the babies had devoted owners. Frances and Kerry enjoyed all the attention. Over half of the pupils at High Woods Primary were keen to find out about the Adopt a Hamster scheme.

The best thing for Frances was the speed with which she made new friends. The adoption forms were shown around and in no time at all dozens of people were asking about Christabel's babies. As soon as the prospective parents were chosen and adults had been consulted about cages and food costs, Frances found that she had five new friends. Hardly a day passed without someone offering news of one of the babies or enquiring about the health of Christabel.

The spring holiday was only one short week away and then Frances and Kerry would be free to do as they liked for two weeks. They could hardly wait.

It was Saturday morning and Frances was lying in bed when the bombshell arrived. It came in the form of a letter which Mum brought into the bedroom.

"Frances, I've got some bad news, love. Poor little Joe has been taken into hospital. He is seriously ill and Aunt Moira is worried sick. Uncle Frank is home but they both need to be at the hospital and so Auntie Moira wants us to have Patrick for the holiday."

Frances scowled and then hid her face under her bed cover.

"Now don't be like that, Frances. That's no way to treat a cousin. You'll have to try to make him feel at home here. After all, it must be a worry to have his little brother so ill. And just as his dad gets home, he's packed off to stay with us."

Mum's speech over, Frances emerged from under the bed clothes. Her wild red hair was sticking out at all angles making her look fierce and slightly crazed.

"I'm not having that toad of a boy spoil our fun, Mum. I'm very sorry for Joe and I hope he'll be better soon but that doesn't mean that Kerry and I have to put up with that horrible pig! I hate him! "

"Frances! Where do you get your language from? That's quite enough of that – rude and selfish you are, and that's the truth of it!"

Mum stalked out of the room and Frances could feel misery settling over her like a cold, damp cloud.

After a brief sulk, Frances dragged herself out of bed. It

was Saturday – her day for cleaning out the hamsters. She still hadn't found a home for Emmeline, the last of the babies. Kerry had hoped to have it but her mum had flatly refused. They had a very lively puppy and Kerry's mum said that that was enough work for anyone. Soon Emmeline would be too old to share the cage with her mother, so Frances was anxious to find her a good home.

The cage cleaning finished, Frances grabbed her coat and asked Mum if she could go and see Kerry. As she dashed down the street, she felt a rush of air and she began to wish that it could grow and grow until it was a rushing whirlwind which would carry off her horrid cousin.

Chapter 3

The first Sunday of the spring holiday was warm and sunny.
Frances helped Mum to prepare lunch for Uncle Frank who
was driving Patrick over from Liverpool. Frances was so
determined that the holiday would be great in spite of
Patrick that she had spent the last few days trying to be
positive about her cousin.

Kerry was quite keen to meet the dreaded boy and so it
was decided that she would drop in, unexpectedly, at about
three o'clock.

Uncle Frank was nicer than Frances expected him to be.
As Patrick adored his father, Frances didn't think she'd like
him. She was wrong. Uncle Frank had stopped at a
motorway gift-shop to buy her a basket-ball. Not the sort of
gooey present that girls were usually given by relatives. She
was especially pleased to learn later that he had taken the
trouble to find out from Aunt Moira that she was good at
games.

Frances and her mum were relieved to hear that little Joe
was doing well after his operation and if everything went to
plan he would be home again the following week. Frances
gave Uncle Frank the get well card that she'd made for Joe
and the pop-up picture book which she'd so carefully
chosen. Patrick curled his lip when he saw the card but
Frances pretended not to notice.

Lunch went well and even Patrick seemed almost human.
He was very quiet and polite and had two helpings of
everything, which pleased his aunt. When the door bell rang,
Frances hurried to answer it.

When she opened the door she was very surprised to find that it wasn't Kerry standing on the door-step, but Chris Berry, a girl in their class.

"Hi, Frances," said Chris. "How's Christabel?"

"Fine," answered Frances. "How's Doolittle? Do you want to come in?" she added.

"No thanks," said Chris. "I've got to dash. I came to say that lambing has started, and I wondered whether you and Kerry might like to call in later and see some lambs being born. A sort of 'thanks' for the hammy."

Chris had adopted the laziest of the babies, which she'd named Doolittle. She lived on a nearby farm and was animal mad. She'd set her mind on becoming a vet and already knew a great deal about animals.

As Frances was asking permission from her mum, Kerry arrived and after a lot of discussion it was decided that the girls and Patrick would go down to the farm later that afternoon.

When Chris had gone and Kerry had been properly introduced to Uncle Frank and Patrick, Mum had a suggestion.

"Why don't you show Patrick the hamsters, Frances? Perhaps he would like to have the last of the babies."

Frances was horrified but didn't say anything. Instead she led the way into the sitting-room where the hamster cage was kept. The girls each took out a hamster and turned to Patrick who was pretending to flick through a magazine.

"Would you like to hold one?" asked Frances, reluctantly.

She need not have worried. The look on Patrick's face said it all.

"No thanks," he said. "I don't like rats. My dad says that those sort of things are all vermin. Shouldn't be allowed to be kept as pets. Once some escaped and got into the sewers. Now they're breeding like flies and they've grown enormous

14

– as big as dogs, they are!"

Kerry rolled her eyes and sucked her teeth rudely but she didn't speak. Frances glowered at her cousin. The boy was stupid. He must believe everything anyone told him.

"You don't like animals, full stop!" said Frances. "I suppose you think the world was made for your benefit and blow everything else. Haven't you ever heard of the balance of nature?"

Frances was angry. She wasn't sure whether Patrick was winding her up or whether he was really a total blockhead. She could feel the rage building up inside her. She was about to start on him again when Mum called.

"Patrick, come and say 'Goodbye' to your dad. He has to go now, love."

Patrick hurried out of the room.

"Wow!" said Kerry. "Talk about biting his head off!"

Suddenly Frances laughed. She had an image of Patrick running around like a headless chicken.

"He's a cowardy-custard!" she said. "He's frightened to hold the hamsters. That's why we got all that rubbish about rodents as big as dogs!"

"Should we go to the farm now?" said Kerry, changing the subject. "It's almost four o'clock."

Chapter 4

It was past four o'clock by the time Frances, Kerry and Patrick set off for the farm. Patrick was dragging his heels at the thought of going out with the girls but his Aunt Geraldine was determined that he should go along and enjoy himself.

"The fresh air will bring roses to your cheeks, young man," she said. "A spell in the country will do wonders for you and then when you go home to your mum she won't recognise you. Run along now and watch the lambing, Patrick. The girls will take good care of you."

Patrick looked like thunder but didn't dare argue. Fifteen minutes later, as they turned a bend in the lane, they spotted Chris sitting on a five-barred gate, waiting for them.

"Hi! You're in luck – my favourite ewe hasn't lambed yet," said Chris. "I'm hoping it's going to be soon. Dad thinks that she might have twins."

The three girls hurried on but Patrick trailed behind. Chris stopped and waited politely but she was desperate to see the twins being born.

"What's that noise?" asked Patrick, as a volley of gun-fire echoed faintly around the farm buildings.

"Oh, it's only my brothers. There isn't much to do on the farm at the moment as lambing has only just started, so they're clay pigeon shooting up on Forty Acre Field. I'll take you up there later, if you like, but please hurry now."

For the first time that day, Patrick looked lively and even quickened his step so that he caught up with Frances and Kerry. As they entered the barn, they were greeted by a chorus of "baas".

Low fencing divided the barn into seven or eight separate pens, leaving a narrow gangway down one side. In each sheep fold there were between eight and ten pregnant ewes. Chris led her friends to the far end and pointed to a sheep lying in the corner.

"That one's Rosie."

Rosie's sides were bulging like saddle bags and she looked very uncomfortable. With mournful eyes she gazed at her visitors.

"How do you know when it's going to happen?" asked Frances, curiously. "Surely they don't all have their lambs at once."

"No! Thank heavens! But it can be a rush," said Chris. "Most lambs are born at dawn; that's the best time because it gives the ewe the maximum amount of sun-light and warmth to get her lamb started. But it doesn't always happen like that, though.

"Rosie is definitely going to lamb soon. Look – she's made a sort of bed in the corner, and when Andy came round with the feed she didn't hurry over like the others."

They all stared at the ewe, which had made a sort of nest in the straw that covered the floor of the barn. Other ewes were moving around and feeding from the troughs but Rosie was ignoring them all. Occasionally, she would glance round at her tail-end, expectantly.

"She's a very experienced mother," said Chris, proudly. "This is her third lambing season. Rosie had to be hand reared when her own mother rejected her. Sometimes, when ewes have triplets they can't manage all of them and if a lamb doesn't have its mother's smell on it, because it's wandered off and got mixed up with the others, the mother won't accept it. If that happens we try to get one of the other ewes to be a foster-mum, but that doesn't always work, either.

"Rosie lived in the farmhouse with us for ages. I used to bottle-feed her. Then Gran came to to stay. She put her foot down. Said it wasn't nice having a kitchen that smelled of sheep, so Rosie had to go out with the others. She still knows us, though."

The girls were smiling across at Rosie but Patrick was standing open mouthed. He didn't know what to make of the idea of having a sheep for a lodger.

Mr Berry, Chris's dad, popped into the barn to say that triplets and a single had been born in the other barn if they wanted to come and look. But Chris said no thanks. She was determined to be present for Rosie's big moment.

She wasn't disappointed. Patrick suddenly said, "Yuk!" and they all looked across at Rosie. There was a rush of birth fluid and then a pair of tiny yellow hooves gradually came into view, pushing out from under Rosie's tail. In another minute a small black nose appeared. Then slither and sloosh! Rosie's lamb was lying on the straw.

"It's not moving!" cried Kerry, in fright.

"Don't worry," said Chris. "It takes a second or two."

Chris was right. The new-born lamb began to lift its head as Rosie warmed and dried it with her rough tongue.

The children were riveted. Every second, the tiny lamb grew more beautiful as its mother licked away the slimy remnants of the birth-sack to reveal its fine woolly coat.

Within five minutes the lamb was bleating softly and in another five it was standing up on its very wobbly legs.

It was Patrick who cried out, "Look! She's having another one!"

And sure enough, Rosie's second baby was making its way into the world. When the soft, wet bundle was lying safe on the straw, Chris's dad leaned over and picked it up.

"Here you are, Rosie," said Mr Berry. "Here's your other baby."

Rosie turned and began to lick the second lamb.

"We'll just check that the milk-bar is all right," he said, "and then we'll leave her to it."

He climbed into the pen and carefully examined the teats on the ewe's udders. Then, satisfied that everything was in working order, he left Rosie and her babies to get on with the first feed.

Frances and Kerry were delighted. The lambs were enchanting and the ewe's care was lovely to see.

After watching the lambs feeding for a while, they went out of the barn and into the spring sunshine. Flopping down on to bales of straw, they let the late afternoon sun melt away the chill of the barn.

Kerry's sigh of contentment brought Frances to her feet. "Where's Patrick?" she asked, suddenly. "He's completely disappeared!"

"I bet I know where he is," said Chris. "Come on, follow me."

Chapter 5

As Chris expected, Patrick was up at Forty Acre Field watching her brothers clay pigeon shooting. Frances felt cross with Patrick but she didn't say anything. Chris introduced everyone to her brothers and Andy, the youngest, showed Patrick how to load, aim and fire the gun. Frances had never seen Patrick looking so happy. They hung around watching the shooting for a while until Frances looked at her watch and said that they had better be getting back home.

"Thanks very much, Chris. It was really great," said the girls in chorus.

Frances stared hard at Patrick.

"Oh, yeah," said Patrick. "It's really good here. Er, thanks again, Andy and Martin."

On the way home Patrick was full of himself.

"Andy says that I can go along on Wednesday afternoon and shoot with them again. He says that I'm really good – for a beginner," Patrick boasted. "Don't suppose you girls would be any good at it, though. Dad says that girls don't have any space awareness."

"You mean spatial awareness," sniffed Kerry. "It's not true, though. My mum says that silly idea goes back to a time when girls were expected to stay at home while their brothers went off into the big wide world to earn a living."

"Like in the fairy stories," chipped in Frances, "where the youngest sons go off to seek their fortunes and fight dragons while the princesses keep house for dwarves or wait in towers and glass coffins to be rescued."

"Yeah," Kerry agreed. "Exciting stuff, eh? Fancy staying

asleep for a hundred years until some soppy prince turns up to kiss you!"

Frances chuckled and then looked serious. "I don't see the point of it, though. Clay pigeon shooting, I mean. I'd rather watch a lamb being born than shoot something out of the sky."

"You're just saying that because they didn't give you a go," sneered Patrick.

"They would have – if we'd asked," said Frances. "We've been to the farm lots of times before, you know. Anyway, what about you? You couldn't even look when the lambs were being born. Mum says that heroes aren't men with guns."

Patrick glowered at Frances and Kerry. What did they know? Stupid girls!

As they drew near to her house, Kerry asked if they would like to go in and see the puppy. Frances had seen it many times before but she loved to hold its roly-poly softness and smell its milky-baby smell.

As usual, Patrick hung back. "Dad says that dogs can carry germs."

"Oh, leave it out, Patrick. Hurry up and don't forget to close the gate!" called Frances as she followed Kerry into the house.

The puppy had grown quite a lot and Frances was surprised to see how lively he was.

"He's very bad about chewing things," whispered Kerry. "Dad's really mad about his new slippers. Patch has eaten the front off one of them."

Kerry looked round for her mother. "Mum, can we take Patch out into the garden?" she called. "We won't be long as Frances and her cousin have to go in a minute."

Kerry's mum agreed and the girls rushed off with Patch yelping at their heels.

Patrick was in the garden lobbing pebbles from the path at a cat which was tiptoeing its way along the garden wall. A stone caught one of its hind legs and sent it yowling off the wall with a frantic leap.

Kerry called out in anger and a woman banged frantically on an upstairs window and shook her fist.

"Thanks very much, Patrick. Get me into trouble!" said Kerry in disgust. "Mrs Porter is loopy about her cat and she'll tell Mum about that."

Frances was silent with embarrassment and Patrick nervously began to kick at the pebbles on the path, sending them shooting off in every direction.

Patch, thinking this was a grand new game, dived at Patrick's feet growling and snarling and nipping at the boy's ankles with his needle-sharp teeth.

The sharpness of the puppy's baby teeth and the mock ferocity of its attack alarmed Patrick. He turned heel and ran for the gate. Patch thought this was a wonderful lark and dashed after him with all the thrill of the chase.

A moment later Patrick's squeals and Patch's yelping were drowned out by the angry screech of brakes. When the girls reached the pavement, they saw a large red van stopped in the road. Lying in front of it, motionless, was a small dark bundle.

Kerry began to wail and Frances spun round shouting, "Beast! Beast!"

But Patrick was already speeding off. How she hated that boy! Her anger overwhelmed her, rushing into her head like a crimson flood. The last thing she remembered, before she passed out, was the picture of two enormous black hounds bounding, hell for leather, after her cousin.

Chapter 6

Frances was worried sick about Patrick. It would be her fault and hers alone if Patrick was hurt. He had been missing for two hours and it was now almost dark. She had let loose those hell-hounds, believing that they were nothing more than phantoms of her imagination, but now her imagination had run away with her. She could see the hounds, teeth bared, chasing Patrick across the countryside. In her anger Frances had wanted to punish Patrick, but her wishes had turned into a nightmare.

Her mum was at the police station waiting for news and their neighbour, Mrs Brown, had come in to sit with her. Frances had taken a while to come round after her fainting attack and the doctor had said that she should be put to bed and kept warm. Frances had wanted to stay up but her mother had insisted that she should go to bed.

An hour ago Kerry had rung to say that Patch was fine. The vet had examined him and there were no injuries. The puppy had been stunned by the blow from the van's bumper but now he was fully recovered. It had even been suggested that Patch's frightening experience with the red van would teach him to keep away from traffic – if he ever got out on to the road again.

Kerry vowed to take more care in future. She should have checked that the gate was properly closed. She was sorry that Patrick had taken all the blame and had run off believing that Patch was dead. She'd asked Frances to telephone as soon as Patrick was found so that she could tell him that everything was all right.

Now that Frances was feeling better she began to think

straight. She hadn't told anyone about the hell-hounds – not even her mum. It was impossible to explain. She had to find her cousin and undo the mischief she had unleashed.

She dressed quickly and tiptoed downstairs. Mrs Brown was watching TV in the sitting room. Pocketing a torch, Frances slipped out of the back door and headed towards the farm.

Half an hour later, as she hurried past the farmhouse and its buildings, she heard dogs barking and thought again of the hounds that she had seen bounding after Patrick.

Frances was very frightened. She began to run, tripping and stumbling over the rough ground. Brambles and briars clawed at her legs and the sappy, lower branches of trees whipped at her face. Frances accepted the pain like a gift. Inside her head lingered the foolish idea that if she was hurt it might somehow save Patrick. Each breath she took was sharp and stabbing but worst of all was the feeling that she was too late.

Clouds shrouded the moon and the night was very dark. A chill mist rose from the damp ground. Her throat hurt and she gasped and coughed as she ran. The dizziness she had experienced earlier began to return. She had to keep alert. Close to the boundary of the farm was a disused quarry. She wasn't sure how close but it couldn't be far away. Above the noise of her troubled breathing she became aware of something following her. She couldn't mistake that sound. It was the excited yelping of tracker dogs crashing through the undergrowth. Perhaps the hounds had missed the trail and, somehow, she had got ahead of them. She had to reach Patrick before the hounds did.

The track she had been following petered out on to ground which was open and stony. There was a brief gap in the clouds and a large silver moon sent shadows jigging like puppets in a magic-lantern show. Frances paused to glance

behind her and the blood froze in her veins. As she stumbled and fell, an image of slobbering jaws and yellow, flashing eyes swamped her mind before a huge shape blacked out the moon.

Mum didn't say very much when Mrs Berry brought Frances home. She was glad that her daughter was safe but she couldn't understand why Frances had decided to go out alone to the woods to look for Patrick.

"Did you two fall out or something, Fran?" asked Mum. "I can understand you being upset about the puppy but why did Patrick feel he had to run away?"

Frances began to cry. "It's all my fault!" she wailed. "I wanted something horrible to happen to him and it has."

"We don't know that, Frances. Patrick may be ..."

Just at that moment the telephone rang.

Chapter 7

Patrick was shocked. As he ran, the noise of Patch's yelp, the van braking and Frances screaming "Beast!" rang in his ears. He didn't want the puppy to be dead.

After fifteen minutes' running, the stitch in his side forced him to slow down and he realised that he was lost. The houses looked gloomy and unfriendly in this part of town and the few passers-by stared at him as if they knew everything about him and his crime. He turned down an alleyway and hurried on, not knowing where he was going.

The alley was deserted. It smelled of cat, and rubbish was strewn down its length. He'd really messed things up this time! If only he could go home to Mum and Dad and Joe. But there wasn't anyone there. They were at the hospital waiting for little Joe to get better. For the first time since he'd been whisked off to his cousin's, he thought of Joe. What if he didn't get better?

I'm a rotten brother, thought Patrick. I only cared about being dumped on Aunt Geraldine; I've hardly even thought about Joe. And now there's trouble here! Everything's hopeless!

He knew that Frances didn't want him here. He'd never go back to that house, to hear those girls saying he was a ... a murderer!

Patrick sniffed and wiped a sleeve across his face. He wasn't going to blubber. Dad said that cry-babies were sissies. He knew how to be hard. He didn't care if everybody did hate him. Tears welled up, stinging his eyes. Again, he paused to wipe his face. He'd show 'em! He'd make them sorry!

When he came out from the alley, Patrick was surprised to find himself opposite the park which they had passed earlier on their way to the farm. In a flash, he knew what he should do.

With barely a glance, Patrick ran across the road. A truck swerved and blew its horn. A torrent of abuse battered his ears but he didn't stop. He wanted to put everything behind him so he just ran.

Ten minutes later, for the second time that day, Patrick was walking down the lane towards the farm. His stitch had come back and he looked around for somewhere to rest. A gateless track led the way into a field and he hurried in and slumped down behind the hedge.

After a few moments his breathing settled into a regular pattern and he felt calmer. It was almost dusk now and he'd decided to make for the shack near the wood. He'd noticed it that afternoon, when he'd taken off in search of the clay pigeon shooters. At the time he'd thought it would make a brilliant gang hut, never dreaming that it would become his hideaway.

Thoughts of home brought back the tears and he felt choked. No one would believe that he hadn't wanted the puppy to be injured. All he'd done was run away from it. If only it hadn't jumped up like that – yapping and snapping and scratching at him with its sharp teeth.

Patrick felt dizzy as the memory flooded back to him – the day on the beach when he was six years old. Dad had bought him an ice-cream cone from the shop near the pier. It was massive – a double sugar cone with strawberry and vanilla ice-cream. Dad had sent him back to stay with Mum while he had a quick pint. Patrick hadn't minded; he knew that Mum was sitting on the beach next to the tall flag pole. He could find the place easily.

He hadn't bargained for the large dog that came

bounding up to him. Afterwards the owner explained that the dog had only wanted to play. At the time, all Patrick could see were the great teeth and salivating jaws of the dog, and the ice-cream cone lying in the sand. When the dog had torn at his swimming trunks, he thought it was going to eat him alive! He still had the scar.

It had been terrible. Worse was Dad's anger. When he returned to them and saw how his son had been attacked, he began shouting about wanting the dog destroyed. But then he'd muttered something slyly as if it was a shameful secret: dog's can smell fear ... they can sniff out cowards ... some people ask to be bitten. Patrick would never forget the shame.

The horror of the memory stung him into action. Patrick leaped to his feet and bolted as if the dog was still on his trail. He had to find the shack!

Stealthily, he skirted the farm without being seen. It was almost dark now so he made straight for the wood, hoping to take a short cut through the wood to the shack. This route meant that the trees would give him cover and it would save quite a lot of leg work.

He was surprised to find how dark it was when he slipped in among the trees but there was still enough light, filtering through the canopy of spring leaf, for him to see where he was going. Ever since he was a small child he'd never been afraid of the dark, and he wasn't now. He had an idea of the direction he needed to head in so he pressed on determinedly to find the shack.

His plan began to fail when he reached the edge of the trees. A stout wire fence blocked his passage out of the wood. Patrick tried to climb over but the wire was new and unyielding. He fell back exhausted, thankful to rest a moment among the dead leaves. Realising that he'd walked too far, he decided to retrace his steps. It wasn't long before

Patrick had to admit to himself that he was hopelessly lost. Fighting back the panic, he plodded on, repeating over and over again under his breath, "I mustn't lose my nerve."

Apart from the sounds of his own footsteps, the wood was eerily silent. The trees themselves seemed to be listening for the small gasps of pain caused by branches scratching at his face. He was walking around in circles. The trees had imprisoned him – there was no escape.

Suddenly, the sharp cry of a frightened animal ripped through the velvety blackness, striking terror into Patrick. Blindly he began to run – then joy! The trees fell away and he found himself speeding across a clearing, the wood behind him. He stopped running but for a split second his body went on flying.

The bush which caught Patrick was hostile with thorns. Despite the scratches and grazes, he clung on for dear life. Below him, in a basin of liquid silver, floated the moon.

Patrick was unsure which way up he was and he struggled painfully to get a firmer grip on the bush. As he tried to gain a foothold, his feet kicked against the wall of the quarry and he heard the splash of stones as they fell into the flooded pit.

Each time he looked down, the moon beamed back at him, inviting him to leave his prickly perch and come to rest on the blanket of silver which was spread out below.

His arms were numb with pain and he longed to let go. Gradually, the tingling feeling crept through his body. Soon it would reach his head and he wouldn't have to go on thinking. His grip relaxed and then tightened. The noise of barking dogs brought him back to his senses. He opened his mouth to scream.

Chapter 8

It was late the next afternoon when Mum and Patrick returned from the hospital. He had been kept in overnight for observation but the doctors had decided that he could go home. There were no bones broken but he looked tired. He had his arm in a sling and Frances stared at it in alarm.

"It's all right," said Patrick, seeing the expression on his cousin's face. "It's only bruised. I can take the sling off as soon as it stops hurting."

"Kerry's puppy is OK," said Frances, all in a rush. "She wanted you to know that it wasn't your fault. I know you don't like animals. We shouldn't have let the puppy jump up at you. His teeth are like razors – but he was only playing!"

Mum smiled wearily. "I think Patrick feels a tiny bit different about animals, now," she said.

Patrick laughed a funny sort of laugh and looked embarrassed. "You won't believe this," he said.

Frances waited. What was it that she wouldn't believe?

"I might have drowned last night – if it hadn't been for the farm dogs, Bodger and Sam.

Patrick continued. "I thought I'd killed the puppy," he said quietly. "I just wanted to go away. I went back to the farm. I'd nowhere else to go. I wandered round for a bit and then hid in the wood. When we were watching Andy and Martin clay pigeon shooting I'd noticed a building on the edge of the wood – just a shack, really.

"It was getting dark and I lost my way. I must have got my sense of direction muddled because I came out of the wood on the side opposite to where I thought I'd be. There's a quarry there – a flooded gravel pit – but I didn't see the edge. When I was running, I slipped and fell. A blackberry bush broke my fall and I hung on.

"Bodger and Sam found me. They'd been barking at something so Andy let them loose. They came straight to me. When Andy and his dad reached me, the bush was hanging out by the roots and Sam was hanging on to the hem of my coat with his teeth. Bodger was barking his head off.

"Another five minutes and I would have been a goner."

"Of course! Sam and Bodger, the farm dogs!" said Frances. "It was me that they were barking at. That's what I saw as I fell. So they weren't hell-hounds that I sent after you."

Patrick gave Frances a funny look.

"I'm beginning to understand," said Mum, shaking her head at Frances. "Didn't I tell you that that imagination of yours would be your bête noire?"

Frances looked puzzled and then she began to laugh. She turned to Patrick. "Mum's little joke," she said. "Bête noire is French for black beast but the expression means something to be afraid of – a kind of pet hate."

"That's a good one," said Patrick. "That's what was wrong with me. I've had a 'pet hate' but I think I might be getting over it now. And tomorrow I'm going to buy some dog treats for Patch and Sam and Bodger."

Moon Madness

Chapter 1

"You can't go, Frances, and that is final!"

Mrs Riley stormed out of the room, slamming the door behind her.

Frances snatched up the plaster of Paris rabbit which stood on the coffee table and hurled it to the floor. There was a soft explosion as it landed on its ears.

Kerry looked down at the mutilated rabbit and then at her friend.

"Frances!" she said, in a shocked whisper. "You shouldn't have done that."

"I know. But I don't care if it is broken," shouted Frances. "I made it for her and now I hate her!"

"Frances!" Kerry was shocked. "You don't mean it. You shouldn't have said all those things about her being mean and you never having any fun. It's not your mum's fault if she hasn't got the money for the holiday. She did say that she likes the idea of an adventure holiday but she just can't afford it."

"Everyone else's parents can afford it!" cried Frances, tugging at her bushy red hair until it stood up like a lion's mane. "It's all right for you," she wailed, "you aren't going to be stuck here all holiday; you'll be off enjoying yourself!"

Kerry squirmed with embarrassment. "Keep your hair on,

Fran. It's not the end of the world."

Frances opened her mouth to reply but decided against it. There was a long, uncomfortable silence.

"I'd better go now," said Kerry, meekly. "I said I'd go straight home after school. Mum'll be wondering where I am."

She wanted to say, "Forget about the holiday ... I'm sorry I suggested it," but Frances was looking so fierce that she didn't dare. Kerry and three other girls from school were planning to go on an adventure holiday in Wales. It had been Kerry's idea that Frances should go with them but Mrs Riley had said no.

Nervously, Kerry chewed her lip; she sort of felt responsible for the row but didn't know what to say. There'd been enough angry words for one day. She didn't want another scene.

"'Bye. I'll see you on Monday," she murmured. And, putting on a brave face, she slipped out of the room, closing the door softly behind her.

As soon as Frances was alone, she bent down and picked up the little rabbit from the floor. Through her tears she could see that one of the ears had broken clean off. She gave a cry of despair. She had been so proud of the little rabbit and now it was ruined. Anger welled up inside her and she snapped off the other ear.

"Oh! oh! oh! oh!" she cried, attacking the cushions on the sofa with clenched fists. "It's not Mum I hate," she wailed. "It's me I hate! I hate me! I always get everything wrong!"

Chapter 2

Frances woke up very early the next morning. Her head ached and she felt wretched. At first she couldn't remember what it was that was troubling her, then memories of the day before came flooding back.

Oh, the shame! She had gone to bed in a huff, refusing anything to eat or drink; refusing, even, to speak to Mum. Although Frances knew that the upset was entirely of her own making, she couldn't bring herself to say sorry. Mum had come in to wish her goodnight but she had pretended to be asleep. She'd held her breath and played possum while Mum kissed her and smoothed her hair, but as soon as Frances was alone, she'd cried herself to sleep.

Frances threw back the duvet and crept out of bed. A large orange sun was just emerging from out of the dense mist which hung like a vapour trail over the valley. Looking out on such a beautiful morning, Frances decided to go and see Chris at Harefield Farm. Days began early at the farm and Frances was sure that her friend would make her welcome.

Quickly, she dressed in jeans and a sweater. But where were her trainers? Every day Frances had to search for them. The mess under her bed was reaching crisis point but she did her best to ignore it. Kneeling down and peering into the muddle, Frances retrieved one of her trainers by tugging at a lace which was snaking out between piles of books and games. The other trainer was more difficult to find. After a few fretful moments, Frances discovered it behind the waste-paper basket. She wrinkled her nose as she removed a mouldy apple core and a wodge of chewing gum from inside. Slipping it on, Frances tiptoed noiselessly downstairs.

Mum was still in bed so she had the kitchen to herself. She made herself a giant marmite sandwich and began to scribble a note for Mum. As she wrote "I'm sorry," she thought again about the lost holiday. A wave of frustration made her crumple up the note and toss it into the waste bin. The disappointment was too much to bear. She wanted Mum to feel really sorry.

Closing the front door as quietly as possible behind her, Frances crept up the garden path and set off for the farm.

The morning mist was lifting by the time she reached the track which led to Harefield Farm. The air was still and there was only the occasional burst of bird song to remind her that she wasn't alone under a vast blue canopy of sky. It felt eerie to be up and about so early in the morning and the strangeness set Frances tingling with a nervous excitement.

The lane ahead was in deep shadow. Tall trees lined both sides of the road, meeting overhead to form a dense canopy of leaves through which the sun was unable to penetrate. Frances hesitated and then forced herself to enter the tunnel of shade. It was cold out of the sunshine and she quickened her pace.

Suddenly, there came a sound which froze her blood. Frances started like a frightened rabbit as a piercing cry, like a child's scream, shattered the quiet of the morning, sending a colony of rooks cawing into the air.

The noise had come from beyond her, on the other side of the trees. What on earth could it have been? Plucking up courage, she moved off, running down the lane towards the first gate and sunlight.

Breathing heavily, she climbed onto the gate. Some distance away, in the far corner of the field, she saw a figure. She couldn't be certain but she thought it looked like Chris's

elder brother, Martin. Was he in trouble? She decided to go and see if he needed any help.

He seemed OK, so Frances presumed that the horrible scream had not come from him. He must have heard it, too, for he was striding purposefully towards some trees which bordered the field. She hurried after him but hesitated when she saw that he was walking towards three men who were standing with a pair of dogs at the edge of a small coppice.

Not wanting to interfere but still wondering about the scream, Frances paused long enough to see one of the men step forward and let fly at Martin with a punch. In one swift movement, Martin fell to the ground.

Frances shrieked with all her might, sending the rooks screaming into the air once more. The man ducked as her cry hit him like a box on the ears, then he turned and fled, with the other men in hot pursuit.

When Frances reached Martin his nose was pouring blood. In his hands he held the mangled corpse of a hare. Frances stared at the soft bundle of brown fur which was torn and streaked with blood. The sound of its scream came back to her and she felt her stomach churn.

"It's a doe," said Martin, in a shaky voice, "and she's in milk. That means there are leverets around. They'll starve to death without their mother. Some people are sick!"

Martin looked at Frances as if he'd only just noticed that she was there.

"What are you doing here, Fran?" His voice bubbled, through the stream of red which was trickling into his mouth.

Frances shrugged, and fumbled for a handkerchief. She was too upset to answer.

"Come on," Martin winced. "I need to get home."

It was only a short walk to the farmhouse and soon Frances was sitting with Chris and her family in the kitchen of Harefield Farm, watching Mrs Berry bathe Martin's nose. Efficiently she cleaned away the blood, before applying cold compresses to reduce the swelling. As she worked, Mr Berry stomped around the room, waving his arms about and threatening the culprit with fearsome consequences.

He had every reason to be angry. Minus the blood, Martin's face looked only slightly less alarming than before. It was the colour of red brick and very swollen. To make matters worse, one of his eyes was disappearing under a podgy mound of dark-purple flesh.

"Calm down, Bill," said Mrs Berry to her irate husband. "This isn't helping Martin one bit. If you're going to drive him to the hospital, you'll need to simmer down. Now, Martin, tell us again what happened."

"I've told you," said Martin, through clenched teeth. "Half an hour ago I was up on the Top Acre. I'd been watching a barn owl feeding when I spotted some cars parked over on Ted Parr's land. I thought it was a bit odd so I walked over there. I'd got as far as Three Corner Wood when some blokes appeared with a pack of greyhounds. All but three of the men and a kid went off towards the cars when they saw me. I watched the dogs put up a hare and go after it; then I followed them as far as the bottom copse.

"The dogs had finished off the hare by the time I caught up with them. Two of the blokes hung back when I appeared but the third started to walk past me as if I was invisible. I said, 'Excuse me, do you know that you're trespassing?' and he said, 'Do you know that you're a squirt?' and he punched me. Knocked me flying! Frances saw him do it. She screamed blue murder."

Martin was trembling with pain and shock, and after he'd changed his blood-stained T-shirt, his mum made him get into the Land Rover with instructions to Mr Berry to take him straight to the casualty department at the local hospital.

41

She was going to ring the police.

The girls watched as Martin and Mr Berry drove off and then Chris took her friend's arm and led her back into the kitchen.

"So what brings you here so early, Fran?"

Frances sighed. "I'd almost forgotten in the excitement," she whispered. "I've sort of run away. Well, not exactly. Yesterday, after school, I had an awful row with Mum. Kerry heard it all. She came home with me to see whether I could go on that holiday we were talking about at school.

"Anyway, I can't go. Mum hasn't got the money. I threw a wobbler. Kerry must think I'm awful! I said horrible things to Mum and, afterwards, I wouldn't speak to her. I was in a mega huff.

"I woke up early this morning, so I came straight here without telling Mum where I was going. I'd better give her a ring – if that's all right. She'll be ever so worried."

"Of course you can," smiled Chris. "You are a dip-stick, flipping your lid over a holiday that costs more than its worth."

Frances nodded in agreement.

Just then, Chris's mum came back into the kitchen.

"Are you all right, Fran dear? You look very pale. Martin said that you've had quite a shock. Seeing all that blood before breakfast can't be good for anyone. Chris hasn't had her breakfast yet and, if you could manage a bite to eat, I'm sure it would do you good."

"What happened was horrible," admitted Frances, sighing, "and it does seem ages since I've eaten."

Mrs Berry smiled and began to busy herself in the kitchen.

"Mum, can Fran use the phone, please? There's something she's forgotten to tell her mum."

"Of course. You know where it is, love."

Chris winked at Frances as she went off to use the

telephone. "Confess to being the incredible sulk and say you're sorry," she hissed.

Frances grinned and stuck out her tongue. She knew what to say without Chris having to tell her.

After Frances had made her peace with her mum and she and Chris had eaten a big breakfast, Mrs Berry had a suggestion.

"Chris has been telling me about your holiday, Frances. Why don't you come and spend a few days here, with us? Chris would enjoy your company and you'd find plenty to do."

"Please, Fran. It would be great," coaxed Chris.

Frances didn't have to speak. Her enormous smile said it all as she nodded, vigorously.

"Thanks! I'd love to. But I'll have to ask Mum first, of course."

Chapter 3

After clearing away the breakfast dishes, Frances and Chris made their way to the barn and climbed the tall ladder which led up to Chris's hideaway in the hayloft.

Frances gave an excited "whoop" as she flung herself on to a pile of straw.

"I love this place, Chris, it's so secret and cosy. I can hardly believe that I'm going to spend a holiday here! I expect that it will be OK with Mum. Can we come to the hayloft every day? And see the sheep and feed the chickens and the pigs? I love pigs ..." she paused. "Thanks for inviting me, Chris, you're the best kind of friend."

Embarrassed by her speech, Frances plunged, head first, into the straw and came out again looking like a demented scarecrow.

Chris laughed. "Hey, never mind the holiday – Dad should pay you to stand up on Top Acre to scare birds!"

Frances leapt to her feet and began flapping her arms, wildly. A shower of straw and dust rained down on Chris.

"Leave it out, Frances!" she cried. "You're a total wally ..."

Encouraged by her friend's squeals, Frances sent more straw flying up until the air was as thick as a bird's nest.

"Who's a wally?" she demanded, thrashing her arms about until Chris looked like a haystack.

"I meant ... you're great fun," wheezed Chris, choking with laughter. "But please, stop!"

Frances stopped fooling around and dived down beside her friend. When her breathing was calm again, she asked a serious question.

"What was going on this morning, Chris? Poor Martin! Your mum says that his nose is probably broken. Why did that man hit him? What were they doing here?"

Chris sighed and looked thoughtful. "Dad's known about the gang for some time. But they've not come on to our land before now. They're hare coursers. They set greyhounds after wild hares. It's illegal but the police don't seem able to stop them. They move about a lot and often they come in quite big groups. Some of the people round here are really scared of them."

"I'm not surprised," said Frances. "What do they do with the hares? Do they eat them?"

"I don't think so." Chris shook her head. "We often find dead hares lying in ditches. The dogs maul them and then they're left to the scavengers. The coursers do it for money. It's a kind of gambling. They bet on the dogs. They come all the way from London and Dad says that there's a pile of money in it. It's no wonder they didn't want Martin spoiling their sport."

"Sport!" cried Frances, scornfully. "Some sport for the hares to be hounded and then torn to pieces by dogs! Oh, Chris, what happened was horrible. You should have seen it ..."

"I know. It's dreadful! Hares are brilliant to watch. The males sometimes have a sort of boxing match. We've found tufts of hair lying on the ground." Chris sighed. "It's not an easy life. Four out of five young hares don't survive. When they're born, the doe moves her litter into a hiding place. Can you imagine spending your whole life on the run, knowing that predators are always after you?"

Frances looked thoughtful. "Chris, do you think that the hare coursers will still be around?"

"I shouldn't think so," answered Chris. "Mum was going to ring the police. They won't hang around if they see a squad car. Besides, if they've sent up another hare they'll be chasing after it. They could be anywhere by now."

Chris noticed how disappointed Frances looked.

"Come on, I know what you're thinking. We can have a walk up to Top Acre, if you like."

"Yes, let's!" said Frances, jumping up. "I'd like to get a closer look at those men."

"It's likely to be a wild goose chase," laughed Chris. "I'll tell Mum where we're going and we'll take Sam and Bodger. No one will give us any trouble if they're with us."

Frances grinned. She had every reason to have confidence in Sam and Bodger. They'd proved their worth once before.

It took the girls twenty minutes to reach the field where Martin had first seen the hare coursers. It was called Top Acre because it lay on the boundary of the Berry's farm and the Parr's. The land was fairly flat here and for some distance they could see empty fields stretching ahead of them. To their left was a small wood and immediately beyond that was a rough track which ended abruptly at a heavy iron gate.

"I guess they've scarpered," sighed Frances, looking around.

"That's where the cars would have been parked early this morning," said Chris, pointing to the track. "It leads to Ted Parr's farm. He lives about three miles further on.

"Let's walk as far as the wood to see if we can find any clues. Then we'll go back the way we came."

As the girl's approached the wood, Sam and Bodger ran on ahead. They disappeared into the undergrowth and began whining and barking and growing more and more excited. The girls looked at each other in alarm. Perhaps the men were still around! Chris called to the dogs. Sam appeared briefly before darting back into the undergrowth which edged the wood.

"I'd better go and see what they're after," said Chris, nervously. "It might be just a rabbit or something."

Frances stuck with her friend and side-by-side they cautiously approached the wood where the dogs were still barking excitedly. They were blinded for an instant as they entered the dense shade of the trees for the wood seemed as black as night. But as their eyes became accustomed to the dimness they saw that the dogs were not very far ahead.

"Sam! Bodger! Here boys!" called Chris.

The dogs either didn't hear Chris or they weren't heeding her for they went on barking and growling at something or someone in the heart of the wood. Frances and Chris hesitated, not sure whether they should venture further into the gloom or stay where they were. The barking dogs were making them feel jumpy. Frances was just about to suggest that they turn back when she felt a heavy hand on her shoulder. She let out a screech as a voice boomed in her ear.

"Boo!"

"Andy! I'll murder you!" Chris snapped, as she turned to find her youngest brother standing behind them.

Frances' squeal gave Chris quite a turn and brought Bodger and Sam yapping round their heels.

"Oh, crumbs!" gasped Frances, shaking with a fit of the giggles, "I thought you were ..."

"One of the baddies?" tittered Andy, enjoying his joke. "I came to tell you that the police have rounded up the gang and they've taken them away. "Mum said you were coming up here so I thought I'd give you two a little surprise."

"You beast!" muttered Chris, as she followed her brother out of the wood. "I'll fix you. That wasn't funny, I nearly had a heart attack!"

"What about me?" said Frances, indignantly. "When he put his hand on my shoulder, I almost fainted."

"Well," chortled Andy, retrieving his old push bike from

the bush where he'd dropped it, "I've got things to do. I'll leave you to decide who's had the biggest scare."

Crowing in triumph, Andy rode off down the bumpy track.

"Right, Fran," said Chris. "We're going to give that brother of mine the fright of his life."

Chapter 4

Chris explained her plan to Frances as they made their way back to the farm.

"If your mum will let you stay tonight," said Chris, hurling a stick for Sam and Bodger to chase, "we can play a brilliant trick on Andy."

"Great, let's do that!" exclaimed Frances, enthusiastically. "I'll ring Mum, and ask." Frances paused. "I wish I hadn't been so horrid to her yesterday."

"Well, give her a ring and ask if you can stay the night. We can go to your house this afternoon to collect your overnight things. If you like, we can take your mum a bunch of lilac. We've got two massive bushes in the garden and it smells lovely."

Frances laughed. "You're a real peacemaker, Chris. You should be a diplomat instead of a vet. I expect that's why animals like you, because you're calm and placid. My temper gets me into awful bother."

"I'm not that placid. And if there's anything that riles me," warned Chris, her voice dropping to a whisper, "it's Andy when he starts his teasing."

"I think he's great," broke in Frances.

Chris flashed her a scornful look. "Girls who don't have brothers always say that! You should try living with him."

"Well, I'm going to, aren't I? If the holiday comes off."

"Just you wait and see. Andy isn't as sweet as you think. He has this monster claw which he bought from a joke shop. It's sort of furry with long talons. It's vile!" Chris pulled a face. "The boy's a walking horror comic – he keeps putting the wretched claw into my bed for a joke. I know that it's only made of rubbery stuff but it gives me a horrible shock when I go into my room at night and find it lying on my pillow!"

Frances laughed. "Before we do anything else, I'd better make that phone call."

Frances soon returned smiling from the hall and sat down at the lunch table. Her mum had given her permission to stay the night which meant that 'Operation Andy' could be put into action.

Martin and Mr Berry returned from the hospital in time for lunch. Martin's nose was still very sore but the doctor had given him something to ease the pain so he was feeling more comfortable.

While they ate, talk centred around the hare coursers. Both Mr Berry and Martin were glad to hear that they'd been rounded up by the police.

"How many men were involved?" asked Mr Berry.

"It seems there were seven in all," answered his wife. "Ted Parr telephoned this morning after seeing the police cars, and I told him what had happened. Apparently he'd seen three cars up on his land early this morning, but they soon moved off, so he did nothing about them."

"Did the police get the kid who was with them?" asked Martin.

Mrs Berry frowned. "There was no mention of any child," she said. "The police officer said there were seven men involved and they were satisfied that that was all."

Martin looked puzzled. "That's odd. I thought I told you this morning. There was a young lad with the three men near the bottom copse. Did you see him, Frances?"

Frances shook her head. She'd seen no boys. She glanced across at Chris who was listening with interest.

"He must have legged it," said Martin. "But now I come

to think of it, I didn't see him running after the others. Perhaps he didn't belong with them, but that seems unlikely."

"Lucky for the men that the police caught them and not Frances and our Chris," laughed Andy. "I caught them playing detective this morning. I reckon they were after somebody's blood."

Chris scowled at her brother from across the table and gave Frances a knowing nudge with her foot.

"So you reckon we're after somebody's blood, Andy? You might be right," nodded Chris, with a saccharine smile.

Frances almost choked, trying not to giggle. She couldn't wait for tonight. They were really going to turn the tables on Andy.

"What did you think of that, Fran?" asked Chris later as they walked down the lane towards the town. "There was a boy with the hare coursers and he's disappeared. I wonder what happened to him."

Frances looked at her friend in surprise. "We're being stupid, Chris! We know what happened to him! When we were in Top Acre Wood, Sam and Bodger were barking at the missing boy. It's obvious. We would have caught him if Andy hadn't distracted us by turning up when he did."

"Should we go and look for him now?" suggested Chris.

"I think I'd better go home for my things," said Frances. "I told Mum we'd be over straight after lunch. I don't want to be in any more trouble.

"If we hurry, we can be back here in an hour," she added. "If he's still around, we'll find him."

Chapter 5

It was early evening and Frances and Chris were sitting in the hayloft staring at a collection of sweet wrappers and a plastic spud-gun.

"Here's the proof that the boy was in Top Acre Wood," said Chris, "but where is he now?"

"Harefield Farm is a spooky place to be after dark," said Frances. "Do you remember Patrick and the gravel pit? He was lucky not to be killed. It was terrifying. Did I tell you about the hounds of darkness?"

Frances laughed nervously but a shiver ran down her spine at the memory.

"Hounds of darkness," echoed Chris. "I expect that's how hares feel about the coursers and their dogs. But now one of them is on the run ... and he's only a boy."

"Chris, do you think that he's in danger?"

"From the gravel pit, d'you mean? The fence has been mended but we ought to try to find him. How do you fancy a real live game of hares and hounds, Fran? But first," grinned Chris, "we have to sort out Andy."

As she spoke, Chris pulled out a large inflatable skeleton from under a pile of straw. Frances giggled as Chris made the grinning skull nod and wave its bony hand.

"While Andy is watching television, we'll pop T Bone Esquire," the skeleton made a low bow, "into his bed, and then we'll go and hunt for the missing boy."

"But no giggling, Fran!" ordered Chris, sternly.
"If Andy hears you, he'll know that we've been up to something."

Martin and Andy barely looked up from the television set when their sister announced that she and Fran were going to play outdoors for a while. Martin nodded and then, remembering his responsibilities as official minder, told them not to stay out too long.

"Don't forget that Mum and Dad will be back from the cinema by ten. You're to be in by then," warned Martin.

"OK!" cried Chris and Frances together. "See you then!"

A few minutes later, Chris led Frances and the dogs out of the farmyard and along the track which ran along the back of the farm towards the gravel pit.

It was a beautiful evening, clear and warm, and the girls were brimming over with excitement as they hurried along under the silvery moon.

"What if we find him and he turns violent?" whispered Frances, anxiously. "If he enjoys blood sports he must be a pretty horrid person."

"He can't be that bad, he's only a boy," answered Chris, but there was a note of doubt in her voice.

The girls were walking down part of the track which snaked through a coppice of trees and for a while the moon was hidden. Bodger and Sam were darting about, sniffing and whining with pleasure, enjoying their unexpected evening walk.

"Ouch!" cried Chris, stumbling over a stone. "Shine the torch on the path, Fran. I can hardly see where I'm going."

An owl shrieked, sending Frances scurrying over to Chris. She grabbed hold of her friend's arm and clung to it.

"Hang on to me," she hissed. "If we stick together, we can see better."

Slowly they crept down the track, plodding after the excited dogs, each secretly wishing that they could turn back.

"Nearly out of the trees now," whispered Chris. "We'll have the moonlight again soon."

"Why are you whispering?" giggled Frances, nervously. "There's no one here."

The girls emerged from the shaded track into a clearing.

"What's that over there?" hissed Chris. Fran's heart missed a beat.

Sam and Bodger were standing motionless and alert. Both dogs were pointing their quivering muzzles towards the centre of a large field.

Frances held her breath as she followed Chris's gaze. In the brightness of the moonlight, a creature was lurching and leaping in a wild dance. Twisting and turning in a spiral of silver, a large hare was performing a spectacular ritual. Girls and dogs were cast motionless under its spell, almost as if they were enchanted.

Then, without warning, the hare ceased its performance and sniffed the air. Catching the scent of the intruders, it bounded away across the field. At once the dogs started barking, leaping forwards in pursuit. Sharply, Chris called them off, but for a moment it seemed they weren't going to heed her. Then they faltered and turned in confusion as another cry drowned out the calls of their mistress.

A shrill howl pierced the night air. The girls huddled together with fear. A few metres away from where they were standing, someone was setting up a clamour loud enough to wake the dead.

As suddenly as it began, the noise stopped and gave way to a muffled sob. As if drawn by magnets, Sam and Bodger darted into the undergrowth, overjoyed to find another trail to follow.

Frances relaxed her hold on Chris's arm and laughed nervously. She drew a breath and called, "Come on out. We know who you are."

Sam and Bodger barked in response and Chris had to hush them.

For a moment the barking ceased and then a shaky voice piped up: "'Help! Call off those dogs, will you!'

Frances and Chris stared as a boy of nine or so emerged cautiously from out of the bushes. Despite the mild evening he was shivering with fright and fatigue. He looked dirty and dishevelled after his hours in hiding.

"Me name's Terry and I'm lost," he croaked. "Don't suppose you've seen three men round here, have you?"

"They wouldn't be the men who broke my brother's nose?" snapped Chris, angrily. "If my dad catches them ..."

"Hang about!" cried the boy, near to tears. "It was Charlie what hit 'im, not Ted nor Pauly. They're rough but they wouldn't bash a kid."

"My brother's seventeen – he's not a kid. Somebody, Charlie or whoever, broke my brother's nose because he asked a perfectly civil question. And besides, you were all trespassing and," Chris's voice rose to a shout, "I'm against blood sports!"

The suspense of the last few minutes was beginning to show itself as anger.

"Me too," muttered Terry.

"What you are doing is cruel. It's not sport. It's not even legal. Besides, the hares are ..." Chris stopped talking and stared at the boy. "What did you say?"

"I said, I am too. Against blood sports and all. I didn't want to come here. Charlie made me. I asked me mum if I could stay with her but she said to mind Charlie or else. It's bad for her if I don't do what he says."

Terry sniffed. "I hate it when them hares die slowly, all twitchy and jerky, like. I didn't want to come with them and when the coppers turned up, well, I knew it was time to disappear. And now they've gone off and left me on me tod. How am I ever gonna get back?" he wailed.

Frances and Chris looked at him and then at each other.

"You'd better come back with us," said Chris. "Mum will be home soon – she'll know what to do."

Terry was obviously relieved to be found, but worried about meeting Chris's family. He trailed behind the girls as they headed towards the farm, and as the trio neared the farm buildings he began to drag his heels.

"Your mum won't want no truck with me after what happened to your brother. More'n likely, she'll want to turn me in."

"No she won't!" said Chris, briskly. "She's a very understanding person."

But nothing that Chris said could persuade Terry that her mum wasn't some kind of dragon after his blood.

Chapter 6

Chris put her fingers to her lips as they approached the farmhouse.

"Mum's car isn't back yet and I don't want my brothers to see you before she does," she whispered.

Terry looked alarmed.

"What'll they do to me?"

"They won't do anything. I just want Mum to see you first. Fran, take Terry into the kitchen while I tell Martin that we're back."

"I want to go home," sniffed Terry, as Frances ushered him into the kitchen. "Me mum'll be doing her nut, wondering where I am."

"Is your mum on the phone, Terry?"

"No, but our neighbour is. Old Hatty won't mind poppin' over with a message," said Terry.

There was an awkward silence.

"Where were you when Charlie hit Martin? I didn't see you."

"I was hidin' in the bushes. I saw you – and I heard you holler. Sounded like one of them hares – poor little things."

"I'm glad that you're against the killing," said Frances, thoughtfully. "Hares shouldn't be hunted."

"They're unlucky, though," said Terry, frowning. "At least, that's what Charlie says. If one crosses your path, you'd better watch out – something nasty will happen to you."

Terry turned his pale face towards Fran. "Did you see that one, tonight? Mad, it was. Frightened the life out of me.

60

They're not natural. Charlie's gran told 'im that when she was a girl, a hare used to come and milk her dad's cow. Witches' servants, she said they are."

Frances rolled her eyes in disgust and Terry squirmed.

"'Course, I don't really believe all that. Mum says that Charlie talks a load of codswallop. He's a bit thick but he's a nasty piece of work. Got a right hook like ..."

"We know," snapped Frances.

"Now look here," said Terry. "Don't blame me. I don't want nothin' to do with the geezer. But Mum's too scared to break away and me dad's done a bunk. I don't want to go back to 'im, but I've got to get home ..."

As Terry was speaking, Fran's eyes fell on a large bruise which darkened the right side of his face and she couldn't help feeling sorry for him.

Suddenly, Terry clammed up and Frances turned to find that Chris and her mum had come into the kitchen.

"Hello, young man," said Mrs Berry. "What are we going to do with you? Chris has been telling me about your predicament. I think we'd better try to phone your mum and then I want to hear some more about this Charlie fellow. From what I hear, he sounds dangerous to know. It's high time someone sorted him out!"

Mrs Berry rang Old Hatty on Terry's behalf and left a message for his mother. Ten minutes later, Terry's mum rang the farm and spoke to her son.

"Me mum's comin' to fetch me tomorrow," said Terry, shyly, when he and Mrs Berry returned to the kitchen.

"Well, don't worry, we'll look after you until then," said Mr Berry. "This is a nasty business but I don't suppose any of it is your fault."

Terry looked from Andy to Martin and winced. Martin's face was black and blue and, as Frances watched the expression on Terry's face, she got the feeling that he knew

something about bruises.

"Let's find you something to eat, Terry," said Mrs Berry kindly. "And then we'll sort you out a comfy bed. I expect you're very tired."

Terry managed a smile but his lips were quivering and he was close to tears.

"We'll show you around the farm tomorrow," said Chris, brightly.

"And Chris's brilliant hideout in the hayloft," chipped in Frances. "You must see that."

Terry began to cheer up, especially when Mrs Berry, set down a pile of sandwiches in front of him. "Tuck into those and I'll see if I can find you a biscuit or two. And Andy'll find you a pair of his pyjamas. They'll be too big, but you won't mind that for one night."

Andy went off, quickly followed by Martin who said he was going to bed as he was feeling very tired.

"It's been quite a day," yawned Mr Berry. "Life on the farm is always busy but today has been worse than usual. I'm not surprised that Martin is worn out. I feel exhausted."

"Never mind, dear," said Mrs Berry. "You can relax now. It's time you girls were in bed. You've had a busy ..."

She broke off as a loud yell rang out upstairs.

"Oh, no! Now what?" cried Chris's dad.

Terry looked up in alarm. For some reason Chris and Frances were shrieking with laughter. Before long, he'd worked out why. The kitchen door was thrown open to reveal Andy and a full-sized skeleton dressed in red and green striped pyjamas!